more litanies
for all occasions

more litanies
for all occasions

GARTH HOUSE

Judson Press
Valley Forge

More Litanies for All Occasions
© 2000 by Judson Press, Valley Forge, PA 19482-0851
All rights reserved.

Bible quotations in this volume are from the New Revised Standard Version of the Bible, copyright © 1989 by the Division of Christian Education of the National Council of the Churches of Christ in the United States of America. Used by permission. All rights reserved.

Library of Congress Cataloging-in-Publication Data

House, Garth.
    More litanies for all occasions / Garth House.
       p.   cm.
    ISBN 0-8170-1354-7 (pbk. : alk. paper)
    1. Litanies. 2. Church year. I. Title.
  BV199.L58 H685 2000
  264'.13 – dc21   99-057317

Printed in the U.S.A.
08 07 06 05 04 03 02 01 00
10 9 8 7 6 5 4 3 2 1

In memory of my beloved wife,
Deanna Sara Wallace
1937–1998

contents

LITANIES FOR
THE CHURCH

litanies for
advent

first sunday in advent

lectionary year a

Leader: The hour is getting late. It is well on into the night. At dawn the rivers will flow in peace into the mighty sea. At dawn the nations will flow to the mountain of God to learn God's ways. God's mountain will rise like the sun, exalted above all. Already the cry of the mourning dove and of the crow announce the approach of light and declare the fulfillment of the ancient prophecy.

People: *Now is the time for love to flow among us! Now is the time for reconciliation! Now the opportunity for forgiveness must be seized! Now, today, we must become love for one another!*

Leader: The world goes about its business: rushing about, grasping for what will not fulfill, thirsting for what will not satisfy, seeking for what will not console. God's promises find no echo in the heart of the world but register indifference with a world too busy to be bothered.

People: *Therefore we shall hold the promises of God on behalf of the world for which Christ gave his life. Our love, our faithfulness shall be the leaven that leavens the whole loaf. We shall wait. We shall watch. We shall bear witness. For we are the firstfruits of a harvest much greater than we can imagine.*

Leader: "Peace!" is the word God speaks. Christ has invited each of us into God's peace, and with us, the whole world. For nations shall beat their swords into plowshares, they shall not lift up the sword nor learn war anymore. For God has spoken and sent the Son, the Lamb of God, the Prince of Peace, as a seal to God's promise.

People: *Long before the dawn breaks, we know its coming is inevitable. For we are heirs to the great promise, to the great hope that was given to us in Christ. That hope, that promise, we guard and treasure for the world. For it was not given to us alone, but for all humanity.*

3

Leader: Therefore, during this Advent season, let us walk the paths of love as those worthy of a great and wonderful inheritance, as the first of many peoples who shall say:

People: *"Come, let us go up to the mountain of the* LORD, *to the house of the God of Jacob; that he may teach us his ways and that we may walk in his paths."*[1] *Amen.*

---

1. Isaiah 2:3.

second sunday in advent
lectionary year a

Leader: As God moves toward us through this Advent season, drawing near to our dwelling as a stranger bearing a lantern might approach out of the forest at night, have we looked within to see what God's light will reveal, to see if we are ready to receive God's gifts, if our hearts are spacious enough for the birth of Love?

People: *For the Christ does not judge by what his eyes see or by what his ears hear. The Spirit rests upon him, and he judges by what is within — the secret heart, the soul, the spirit within each of us.*

Leader: The spirit of this age and of these times would bury our inner truth beneath myriad distractions and enticements. The world would have us so busy rushing about that we would not know whether we had prepared within a manger or a dungeon for our approaching guest.

People: *Therefore we shall create a space for peace within us this Advent season, a corner of the soul calm and safe, quiet and tranquil, where a child might choose to walk. We shall make of our soul a sanctuary, a haven, where prayer has a home and thanksgiving an altar.*

Leader: As the household of God's people, we shall prepare to receive our Lord. The peace that is within each of us shall spread among us until we become as silent and receptive as the moonlit forest in winter.

All: *In that silence, in that peace, Love will be born, that all nature might be reconciled. We shall become as a glade deep in the forest, sheltered by the branches of our prayers, silent and tranquil, where the wolf and the lamb, the leopard and the kid, the calf and the lion shall come and together find rest. Amen.*

5

❧ third sunday in advent ❧

lectionary year a

Leader: Within each one of us is a blindness struggling to see, a deafness straining to hear, a lameness longing to be made whole. Perhaps we are blind to our own beauty or deaf to the word of forgiveness or crippled by shame or self-doubt. Each of us, deep within, is broken, less than whole, in need of healing.

People: *How hard we work at concealing our weakness and need from others, from ourselves, and from our God! We wear myriad masks for each other and for the world, and in the end all that is left within is a lonely, wounded child mutely reaching out with empty hands.*

Leader: Like us, the one who gave the blind sight and made lepers clean entered a broken world with the innocence of an infant's cry. A man of sorrows, acquainted with grief, he was broken in every way except in his communion with God. He shares our fragile, wounded frame and knows each scar, each blow we have ever received.

People: *To be known so intimately, so deeply, is to be loved with an immeasurable love! We believe, O God; help our unbelief!*

Leader: Help us to cast aside the false mask we present to you, to open the gate to our anxious hearts that the Healer might gain entrance and lay gentle hands upon us.

People: *Because he entered our world, shared our lot, gave his life on the cross, the whole world now sojourns toward one great healing.*

Leader: In him each of us can find the wholeness for which we long. As we prepare for the birth of God, for the birth of love, for the birth of healing, let us open our hearts for the balm that heals, for the hands that make whole, for the Spirit that brings peace.

All: *Our eyes shall be opened and our tongue freed, and we shall sing with joy and leap like the deer. Our souls shall blossom and be glad, and everlasting joy shall be upon our heads. Amen.*

❧ fourth sunday in advent ❧

lectionary year a

Leader: The cottonwoods have surrendered their fragile leaves to the cold breath of December. They lift their barren branches toward wind-polished stars that gaze down in eternal benediction on the world God has visited. The one who dwells in the bosom of God's heart still longs to descend into the souls of those for whom he offered his life, still longs to be born and to find life in the hearts of his lovers.

People: *O that our souls might stand in the simple garments of Mary's humility, that her simplicity and openness might be ours! If we could wait with her patience, accept with her readiness, obey with her joy! Then our Christ would come to the mansion of our soul and make his home with us.*

Leader: Our surrender to God, like Mary's, is not an easy one. But God, like a skillful and tender midwife, even now works secretly within us to prepare us for our spiritual birth, to open our hearts for the descent of the Dove.

People: *What is not possible for us is possible for God. The one who has sown the seed in our hearts has pledged himself to the harvest. We bring our longing, expectation, and desire, and await the coming of the one who loved us first.*

Leader: Therefore let us wait in certain expectation that our longings will be fulfilled, our thirsts will be quenched, and our hungers will be satisfied. Let us stand alert and watchful for God's presence revealing itself in each unfolding moment of our days. For it is truth itself, love, healing, and mercy that are to be born in our hearts this glorious season.

People: *The soul of each of us stands before you, O God, dressed in simple and humble garments, even as peasants might wear before their king.*

7

Leader: Who are we that we should become vessels for your holy light to shine forth into the world? Who are we to bear in our hears, as Mary bore in her womb, the word of love? Who are we to give birth in our souls to the Spirit of healing and peace?

People: *Yet with Mary's simplicity we say to you this morning: Let it be with each of us according to your word. Amen.*

first sunday in advent

lectionary year b

Leader: Where are those who wait for God, who have turned off the chattering static of these times and instead wait with patience in silence for the God who comes to those who wait?

People: *The clamor of life and of the world rises around us every day. From every side, on every front we are distracted, enticed, allured. We race through each day. We collapse in bed each night. We are driven and harassed, but we long for freedom and peace!*

Leader: God's Spirit abides in the midst of hurried lives. God moves with you through the busy distraction of your days. But who abides with God? Who waits upon God as a maidservant waits upon her lord? God is like the beloved, scorned and forgotten by her lovers, yet serving them continually even as they abandon her.

People: *Before all things, before obedience, before deeds, before righteousness, God asks us for our love, for our attention, for our waiting. For the gift God would give us above all other gifts is the gift of God's love, the gift of God's self.*

Leader: Only in silence between the stars above shepherd fields can choirs of angels be heard. Only in still waters can the vision be seen. Only in the hushed chambers of the heart can the Spirit be felt.

People: *O God, you are our creator. We are the clay; you are the potter. Fashion us during this Advent season that we may become vessels in which your peace may abide.*

Leader: Forge our souls into spacious homes where the Christ shall be a treasured and welcome guest. Set us at watch for your approach, O God, and prepare our hearts for joy when you arrive.

People: *For we do not wait for the quaking of mountains or thunder and flame, but for a love as tender as a newborn's wail, as gentle as a mother's calming whisper; in Jesus' name. Amen.*

9

৯ second sunday in advent ৯
lectionary year b

Leader: From the mountain heights the cry goes forth. A song of hope moves through the land. The harmony of expectation stirs our hearts. What is this new sound upon the earth? What is this new word being spoken in our hearts? What is this strange music that rejoices our souls?

People: *Let the scales of habit and weary custom fall from our eyes that we might be open to the new life God is bringing to us. Let jaded and callous hearts be born again that we might not miss the promise that hangs in the air during these holy days.*

Leader: For with tender tread God approaches you, longing to enter your home, your heart, your soul, and therein establish healing and peace. The Spirit desires to overshadow you that Christ might be born anew in your being and his holy light shine through you out into the world.

People: *In stillness and silent waiting can God's softest whisper be heard. Each day is a portion of eternity, each passing moment a unique and sacred opportunity to hear and see God working in our lives. Let us live each day carefully, mindfully, that we may be ready to receive the promised gift.*

Leader: We shall all wither and fade like the grass of the field. The breath of God shall blow upon us, and the earth shall see us no more. Even the earth and all its works and the heavens shall dissolve and pass away.

People: *Yet we are hidden in God, each of us a word flowing from the Most High. And the word of our God shall stand forever.*

Leader: The one who is in the bosom of God has visited us, dwelt in our midst, shared our transient frame. He is the guest we await with hope and with joy, the child for whom we create a shelter in our hearts, the gift whose coming is promised anew each day of our lives.

People: *Let us not be afraid to allow our expectations their full measure of hope and joy. Let us lift up our voices with the prophet and cry: "Prepare the way of the Lord, make his paths straight."*[1] *Amen.*

---

1. Luke 3:4.

☙ third sunday in advent ❧

lectionary year b

Leader: Each morning: a new heaven and new earth. Each day: a new creation to be celebrated. Each passing moment: a new opportunity for black and white, Muslim and Jew, Protestant and Catholic, for every division of animosity in the world to lay aside its hatred and speak the word of peace. If not now, when? If we cannot be the Kingdom now, how shall it ever come to pass?

People: *The Savior came from the bosom of God and entered a world and a land torn apart by division and hatred. The Holy One walked its dusty paths teaching, healing, sowing peace with those ready to receive the word of peace.*

Leader: One man, misunderstood, outcast. One man, ready for obedience, ready for sacrifice, ready to give, with eyes fixed only on God. One man living the Kingdom now, not caring whether the world was ready.

People: *Even now God approaches, moves toward us into the sacrament of the present moment to call us into the way of love. The voice still cries in the wilderness.*

Leader: Even now we must look within to see if we are ready for new life, for the birth of God's radiant goodness in our hearts and the discipline of Christ's gentle yoke upon our souls.

People: *Let us look within and examine our hearts. Let us sweep away the cobwebs of selfishness and despair that choke our desire for newness of life. Let us wash the windows of our soul for the inflowing of the light that moves toward us this season.*

Leader: Each day's news announces that nothing has changed in the world. Violence, tragedy, ignorance, hatred — all these still tear the human family apart.

People: *But we are changed. Because Christ has entered our world, we have all received grace upon grace. Among us and within us a new* *heaven and new earth has dawned. The old has passed away and shall be remembered no more.*

Leader: Therefore let us move into the world: one people, ready for obedience, ready for sacrifice, one people with eyes fixed on God, one people living the Kingdom now, not caring whether the world is ready. Amen.

fourth sunday in advent

lectionary year b

Leader: Because we know the whole story, we cannot behold the child without seeing the man. For us, Christ's birth, life, and death are illuminated by the light of resurrection, and in this light our celebration moves into the deeper channels of the heart where joy and grief, exaltation and sorrow resolve into the greater harmony of peace.

People: *The gift of our redemption was prepared and completed for us long before we were born. Our God knew our need before we could ask. The peace that passes all understanding has been waiting for us a long time.*

Leader: Simeon lifts the child from his mother's arms and blesses God. Mary hears his words, both wonderful and ominous. Anna gives thanks and prophesies the redemption of Jerusalem. It is a new beginning for humanity. The glory of God has come to earth, and it is the glory of a newborn child.

People: *God abides in our hearts. God dwells among us. Not in temple stone or church brick can our God be known to us, but in the intimacy of flesh touching flesh is God's love made real.*

Leader: Nathan said to David: "I will raise up your offspring after you . . . and I will establish his kingdom. He shall build a house for my name, and I will establish the throne of his kingdom forever. I will be a father to him, and he shall be a son to me."[1]

People: *What child, what life, what gift is this that opens up eternity, that creates a living body of worship — a new Israel inviting all earth's people into God's promises?*

Leader: God's promise of new life, of the rebirth of hope, is ours this Advent season, sealed in an infant's cry, an old man's blessing, a

---

1. 2 Samuel 7:12–14.

BUSINESS REPLY MAIL

FIRST-CLASS MAIL   PERMIT NO. 6   VALLEY FORGE PA

POSTAGE WILL BE PAID BY ADDRESSEE

JUDSON PRESS

PO BOX 851
VALLEY FORGE PA 19482-9897

Book title: _____

Your comments: _____

_____

Where did you hear about this book: _____

Reasons why you bought this book: (check all that apply) ☐ Subject ☐ Author ☐ Attractive Cover
☐ Recomendation of a friend ☐ Recomendation of a Reviewer ☐ Gift ☐ Other _____

If purchased: Bookseller _____ City _____ State _____

Please send me a Judson Press catalog. I am particularly interested in: (check all that apply)

1. ☐ African American
2. ☐ Baptist History/Beliefs
3. ☐ Bible Study
4. ☐ Children's Books

5. ☐ Christian Education
6. ☐ Christian Living
7. ☐ Church Leadership
8. ☐ Church Supplies

9. ☐ Devotional/Prayer
10. ☐ Preaching/Sermon Helps
11. ☐ Self-Help
12. ☐ Women's Issues

Yes, add my name to your mailing list!

Name (print) _____

Street _____ Phone _____

City _____ State _____ Zip _____

Please send a Judson Press catalog to my friend:

Name (print) _____

Street _____ Phone _____

City _____ State _____ Zip _____

Judson Press • P.O. Box 851 • Valley Forge, PA 19482-0851 • 1-800-458-3766 • FAX (610) 768-2107

widow's prophecy. Let us be open to the fulfillment of God's promises in our own lives.

People: *O God, your promises have always surpassed the narrow imaginations of humanity. Open our minds and our hearts this Advent season that our souls might be wide enough to hold all the love you long to give us; in Christ's name. Amen.*

first sunday in advent
lectionary year c

Leader: Look up and raise your heads, people of God, for your redemption is drawing near! Indeed, your salvation is at hand, for the one who died for you abides in your midst, dwelling in perfect joy within you and among you!

People: *Our God is not a distant god, but one who dwells in intimacy and love with those who create a guest room in their hearts for their creator. God's Spirit dwells more closely with us than we do with ourselves, plumbing the depths of our being and searching out the hidden treasure of our souls.*

Leader: Oceans toss and roar, the nations tremble, the heavens quake, and the frame of this world is forever passing away. The fabric of culture disintegrates, the winds of change blow wild and free, values once cherished are questioned. Yet the one who came only to love abides. The one who came to heal still moves toward us through the days of this holy season. The one who came to liberate still beckons us toward freedom.

People: *The time for love to be born is always now. The time of redemption is always at hand. The sign of the Savior is not in the heavens, but within our own hearts. The evidence of God's presence is not in the roar of the oceans, but in the love we extend to one another.*

Leader: People, let your love abound this Advent season that heaven might rejoice over this colony of heaven. Let your kindness overflow that you may become gentle enough to receive the one who would not lift up his voice or quench a dimly burning wick.

People: *Establish our hearts unblameable in holiness, O God, and let us increase and abound in love for one another and for all persons that we may be ready to receive and welcome the one who comes to us in lowliness and love. Amen.*

second sunday in advent

lectionary year c

Leader: John the Baptist's cry rings in our ears as we are called to turn away from what is passing and trivial, turn away from what is empty and false, turn away from all that does not nourish to eternal life. Our souls must become again a highway simple and straight whereon the one who is truth might make his gentle approach.

People: *O Lord, we confess that the cares and anxieties of this world have threatened to choke the seed you have planted in our hearts.*

Leader: We are burdened with distractions and with desires that call us in many directions.

People: *Let the soft rain of your Spirit fall upon our weary hearts that we may be renewed and made ready to receive the gift you have prepared for us.*

Leader: The one who came among us as one of us brings, not judgment, but compassion; brings not rebuke, but healing; calls down, not the wrath of divine justice, but the peace of divine mercy.

People: *Let us repent, therefore, by casting fear from our hearts and turning with all that is within us to the one who longs for us to know God's love.*

Leader: Let us prepare our souls for the birth of love by casting aside worry and anxiety, finding our peace in trusting the one who is peace.

People: *We have seen the salvation of God walking among us as a servant, healing the broken, lifting up the downcast, bringing light into the darkness. That salvation moves toward us through this Advent season. We gather, like those at the Jordan, to prepare ourselves to receive the gift of rebirth and renewal.*

Leader: Move upon us, O Spirit of God, and purify our hearts like the clear waters of the Jordan, that as we celebrate the birth of healing and love into the world, we ourselves might welcome the one who is love into our hearts and proclaim with the Baptist and the prophets: "The crooked shall be made straight, and the rough ways made smooth; and all flesh shall see the salvation of God."[1] Amen.

---

1. Luke 3:5–6.

❧ third sunday in advent ❧

lectionary year c

Leader: The ancient prophet sings of the day when God would come to dwell with the people of God, abide in their midst, guide them, and free them from fear: "Sing aloud and shout!" he cries out. "Rejoice and exult with all your heart!" he sings.[1]

People: *O that day is ours! We are the heirs to that ancient promise, for in the Christ God entered our world to claim us for his own and to renew us unto eternal life. We are gathered now, our bodies become one body, our hearts one holy temple where the Spirit, like a snow-white dove, rests in utter peace.*

— silence —

Leader: The Word became flesh and dwelt among us, full of grace and truth. He came to his own home, and his own people received him not. They were looking for glory, for power, for freedom, for judgment, but all in terms of the broken human imagination.

People: *O Lord, teach our hearts to know you when you enter our lives, to see you when you cross our paths, to listen in stillness for your voice. As we celebrate this holy season, teach us that for you glory is in lowliness, power in vulnerability, freedom in surrender, and judgment in mercy.*

Leader: For God's ways are not our ways, and God's judgment not our judgment. Jesus brought a light into the world so bright and so good that we shall spend our whole lives understanding how deeply we are loved.

People: *We feel that love among us and within us. Let us seek that love always, moving ever deeper into the mystery of our salvation, cleaving unto the one who gives us the peace that passes all understanding and trusting that he abides with us now and forevermore. Amen.*

---

1. Zephaniah 3:14, paraphrased.

fourth sunday in advent

lectionary year c

Leader: Blessed are they who believe in the fulfillment of what God has spoken of them! Blessed are they whose hearts and imaginations are open and ready to perceive the hand of God in their lives!

People: *For our God is a God of surprise, of unexpected joy, of goodness breaking in upon us suddenly like a dayspring from on high.*

Leader: One day follows upon the other, and at times it seems that there is nothing new under the sun. But for those who walk in the Spirit, all things are continually being made new.

People: *The world goes about its business, buying and selling, but for us who are called out of the world, we move through this holy season breathless with joy and expectation, traveling with Mary to the hill country and hearing Elizabeth's words with a wonder and excitement as new and fresh as the first snows of winter.*

Leader: For love must be born now, today — born and born again within us and among us. The Christ must enter our world today, speak with *our* voices, embrace with *our* arms, heal with *our* love. God's peace must break again upon the world through the fellowship of peace we create here among us.

People: *O let us become like Mary — our hearts open and ready to receive the word of God's love, love so impossibly good, so beyond our highest hopes, so full of gentle honoring that our souls must, like Mary's, break into songs of praise:*

All: *Our souls magnify the Lord, and our spirits rejoice in God our Savior, for God has looked with favor on the lowliness of his servants. The Mighty One has done great things for us. Holy is his name!*[1] *Amen.*

---

1. Luke 1:47–49, paraphrased.

litanies for
lent and easter

first sunday in lent

Leader: After the water and sunlight of the Jordan, after the Spirit had rested on Christ like a dove, after God's embrace had lifted him with a strong and mighty assurance — after all of this, then followed the wilderness, the treeless wasteland of rock and empty sand, the nights of bitter cold and the days of silence and burning heat and hunger. A voice, friendly, genial, came to him: "Young man, if you are the Son of God, turn these stones to bread."

People: *"It is written: 'One does not live by bread alone, but by every word that comes from the mouth of God.' "*[1]

Leader: Again the voice, friendlier now: "Young man, if you are the Son of God, cast yourself down from the parapet of the temple. Surely God's angels will protect you. Surely you are an exception to all men. Surely God would not see you vulnerable to the common dangers of this world."

People: *"Again it is written: 'Do not put the Lord your God to the test.' "*[2]

Leader: And then the voice again, persuasive, enticing: "Behold, young man, do you see the mighty kingdoms of this world, the riches and the glory? Who more fit to rule than you? Who more worthy of the scepter than yourself? Only worship me and they shall be yours!"

People: *"Away with you, Satan! for it is written, 'Worship the Lord your God, and serve only him.' "*[3]

— silence —

Leader: Behold your Lord, people of God. He would not give you bread that does not nourish to eternal life. He would not hold himself aloof from the common lot of all flesh, even unto death. He would not give you a kingdom that was not from the hand of his God.

1. Matthew 4:4.
2. Matthew 4:7.
3. Matthew 4:10.

People: *It is he who has called each of us here this morning, gathered us from out of our lostness into the illumination of his work.*

Leader: Sing, angels of grace, of the Good Shepherd, the one who would not flee but walked steadily and fiercely into the gaping maw of temptation. He was tested in every way yet did not sway or fall away from the work of God.

People: *Lord, in ourselves we are weak and in need. Temptations press hard on all sides. We struggle, we search, we fight, but finally we can only throw ourselves on your grace, seeking your strength and not our own.*

Leader: Listen, O people, for even now the risen Christ speaks: "Come unto me, you who are afraid and hard pressed. Let me take your hand and lead you forward. Share in my life as I so long to share in yours. For I know the enemy, and I have placed the enemy under your feet. Rejoice, for victory is mine, and victory is yours!"

People: *Precious Lord, take our hands; lead us on to the promised land of joy. Let us join you on the road to Jerusalem. If we are lost, you shall find us. If we flee, you shall seek us out. Even if we abandon you, you shall never abandon us.*

All: *Let us reach out to one another and make our ascent to Jerusalem. Christ abides with us on our journey and goes before us in victory. Precious Lord, take our hands and lead us onward. Amen.*

❧ second sunday in lent ❧

Leader: O God! Hear with patience the confession of your people:

People: *We have withheld so much from you. We have hidden our lamps under tables; we have buried our talents out of fear; we have sought security in everything but you.*

Leader: In the gifts you have given us out of your love, we have seen, not the evidence of that love, but instead the false reflection of our own self-importance.

People: *Open our hearts as we follow your Son on the road to Jerusalem that we might comprehend your unchanging generosity, for you have withheld nothing from us.*

Leader: When Abraham lifted his eyes and saw the mountain in the distance, he did not slow his stride; he did not hesitate. The love that called him forth from his native land, the love that promised him a future as infinite as the star-flung heavens, the love that befriended him and called him to trust, that unfailing love climbed with him on the slow ascent to the place of sacrifice.

People: *We are called to sacrifice our narrow expectations and empty our grasping hands to receive the goodness our God longs to give us.*

Leader: Those who followed Jesus on the road thought they knew what they wanted from him. Yet on the cross they found their expectations shattered, only to receive in the rainbow of the resurrection a gift surpassing the furthest reaches of their imaginations.

People: *Each of us has traveled with the Lord. We have in our own way experienced the burning bush, the pillar of fire, the ashes of spiritual exile, the hands of healing love, the dawn of resurrection, the word of promise in a star-filled night.*

Leader: Sustained thus far on our journey by the love that strengthened Abraham, let us cast our distrust of the future aside and go forward with courage and confidence.

People: *The one who loved us first while we were yet enemies to love calls us to throw aside the heavy burden of the self. Would that we could do this on our own, by our own power, through our own wisdom! But we cannot, for salvation belongs to God.*

Leader: Help us, O God, as we journey with your Son toward Jerusalem. In your love is the promise that even in our ascent, even on the way, springs will break forth for us and the Spirit will guide and nourish us. The rainbow of your promise rests behind us while before us the light of resurrection rises like the spring from fallow earth.

People: *The ashes and the dust, the darkness and confusion that are also part of our sojourn — these we can bear when you walk so closely by our side.*

Leader: I hear the sound of lutes and tambourines! A slow and graceful dance has broken out among the people of God! A festival of light has dawned on a people called to go forth with the joyous step of victory already won. For God has given the people everything they need for their journey. God has withheld nothing, not even God's fragile heart, not even the Son, who now in gentleness leads his people forward. Return unto your rest, O my soul, for the Lord has dealt bountifully with you!

People: *Rejoice! For we are not alone in this wilderness of shadow and light. We have each other. We have the Lord in our midst. We have the Spirit binding us together into one household of faith. Trust in one another. Trust in God, for God has provided in the past and will surely provide again. Amen.*

❧ third sunday in lent ❧

Leader: How long the journey is! How far we have come. How often we have found newness of life welling up in our lives like a fountain when we thought ourselves unable to go on. Yet still we doubt the future, still we wonder if the river of our joy has not run dry and the springs of our faith become exhausted in the harsh realities of the wilderness pilgrimage.

People: *Jesus said: "If you knew the gift of God, and who it is that is saying to you, 'Give me a drink,' you would have asked him, and he would have given you living water."*[1]

Leader: O Lord, deep is the thirst of your people. The weariness of life is sometimes too much. Our sins, our sorrows, our griefs dwell closely with us each day of the journey. So many demands are upon us, so many distractions, so many unspoken fears.

People: *Jesus said: "The water that I will give will become in them a spring of water gushing up to eternal life."*[2]

Leader: The rains of spring water the brown earth as a promise fulfilled. The grass sprouts and greens the weary fields of February, and the sparrows return unbidden except by God's steadfast love. The ice breaks on the river, and in the gullies the water sings with the hope of renewal. The earth shall rise reborn and transfigured, for God's promises never fail. God's steadfast love cannot be shaken.

People: *O Lord, give us that water that will end our thirst, renew and strengthen us. Clear our vision to see your playful and majestic hand continually at work in our lives and our world.*

Leader: The future is a land toward which we are called, and we ourselves are a promise fulfilled, a promise spoken long ago to Abraham. As he believed and went forth, so let us cast fear aside and believe the word of our God:

---

1. John 4:10.
2. John 4:14.

People: *That when we ask, we shall receive, and when we seek, we shall find.*

Leader: The star-strewn heavens that Abraham beheld still shine down upon us. The cup that strengthened us in the past is still held out to us in gentleness and love. God's hope and trust in his servants remains as unshakable as the firmament itself.

People: *Let us go forward from this place confident in our God who has led us thus far. The promise that once only hung in the heavens as a curtain of stars has come to us in the presence of Christ Jesus himself, who walks in humble equality among us.*

Leader: It is Christ who calls us onward. It is he who bids us drink and rise to newness of life. It is he who says, "Come, let us go forward." Amen.

❧ fourth sunday in lent ❧

Leader: What a weary place the world can be! Happiness and fulfillment are promised to us from every bookstand, from every chattering television, from every smooth-talking guru who captures our fleeting and wandering attention. We buy, we accumulate, we seek, but if we are honest, we know that our hands are empty, our thirst unquenched.

People: *Jesus said: "Let anyone who is thirsty come to me, and let the one who believes in me drink. As the scripture has said, 'Out of the believer's heart shall flow rivers of living water.'"*[1]

Leader: Behold! The rock from which you have been hewn has been shattered in the wilderness, broken for you, and from it waters of healing and life flow forth!

People: *These waters are pure and rushing, cascading down, flowing without end, pouring over smooth and polished stone, bearing energy and life and sweeping away all that would keep us from newness of life.*

Leader: These waters run deep in the soul, in the still, quiet place within where God waits, eternally patient, for us to come and rest.

People: *These waters abound where gentleness and tolerance shape our relationships, where kindness, acceptance, and forgiveness inform the small, daily gestures that make up our lives.*

Leader: From on high the one who is most holy has entered our world, walked beneath these same blue skies, felt the heat of the sun, known the frailties of our flesh. He has become a fountain of life for his pilgrim people in the midst of a barren world. Like a wild mountain stream, his Spirit rushes around us, sweeping us forward toward rebirth, washing over us again and again to cleanse us from the dust and weariness of our journey.

People: *Let us rest and be restored. Let us drink and be satisfied. Let us wash and be cleansed.*

---

1. John 7:37–38.

Leader: For the one who is the resurrection and the life, the way and the truth, that one is our peace, our protection, our hope, our fulfillment.

People: *The world beckons with its empty promises, shiny and alluring, but we have been chosen out of the world to know the waters of life that truly heal the soul, even Christ Jesus. Amen.*

fifth sunday in lent

Leader: "O LORD, our Sovereign, how majestic is your name in all the earth!"[1]

People: *O that the gentleness of God might reign, that the heavens might pour down the waters of healing upon our earth, this earth too often stained with the blood of violence.*

Leader: Behold: In the white and lavender flowers of spring, in the dark and quiet rains of June, in the mouths of newborn babes cooing like the doves at dawn, in the touch without words upon the shoulder, in the sabbath stillness of the sanctuary — there is revealed God's gentle countenance; there the emblem and the sign of God's overarching power are seen.

People: *We are a people of gentleness. We are children of the delicate sound of summer thunder and the distant waterfall of heaven's nourishing rains.*

Leader: For our God speaks in the eyes of the fawn in the meadow and cries out at dawn in the spiraling cry of the hawk.

People: *The Creator sings in the creeks rushing in torrents, beats out a rhythm in the footsteps of the servants of the Word, paints the image of God's glory with the myriad colors in each day's firmament of glowing light.*

Leader: Would that the prelude to a world ruled by God's love were like the dark and quiet rains of spring, even as the prelude to forgiveness might be the flowing of tears from hearts broken at the sight of God's children shattered by violence.

People: *Would that the prelude to the kingdom of heaven were like the earth's children wakening gently to a dream of poetry and truth, even as the heart of humanity might mature into the gentleness of God's mercy and grace.*

---

1. Psalm 8:1.

31

Leader: For this world of beauty and light is not lacking in the abundance of love. Faith is not rare or scarcely seen beneath these heavens.

People: *Come down, O Lord, and sojourn with your people. Join us beneath these skies we love and walk again across these verdant fields we treasure. Help us, O God, to heal this world you love so much.*

All: "O Lord, our Sovereign, how majestic is your name in all the earth!" Amen.

maundy thursday

Leader: In the ashes of a burned-out church a lark sings as though sorrow had never known the heart of our world. On the river the light dances as though creation had never tasted the brokenness of grief. The rivers run in silver strands and our fields of plenty rise in beauty like the dreams of children untouched by experience. Heavens and oceans turn and swirl with the majesty of the Creator's hand, and the world sings a melody of grandeur.

People: *Ours is the gift of life — of life in abundance. The generous wealth of God is poured forth into our lives, and we are overwhelmed.*

Leader: Yet in the forest the sparrow with broken wings falls and cannot rise. In the evening after the dishes are cleared, a bitter silence falls between husband and wife. A father beats his child, whose heart withers in fear and shame.

People: *In a littered alley hope disappears in the delirium of alcohol. In a cardboard box beneath the overpass hunger and despair join hands.*

Leader: O God, that you might paint the rising mountain peaks with glory, or set the firmament dancing with light, or call forth the myriad creatures of the oceans, or resurrect the dawn with the caroling of birds — these things we can understand.

People: *But at the heart of this world and of ourselves there is a brokenness beyond words. Can you, O God, touch our world in the deepest shadow of this wounding?*

— silence —

Leader: And so, having sung a hymn, the disciples went forth from that place following Jesus as they had for so long. They were small in number, for many had fallen away. They came to a garden, and he was in anguish and did not want to be alone. He asked them to keep watch over him. But they could not, and they fell asleep. He was alone, and it was night.

People: *O Lamb of God who takes away the sins of the world, in you God has known and touched the deepest void of our loneliness. In you God has been one with us at the most radical extreme of our suffering.*

Leader: The innocent man gave himself to the angry mob that came that night. Into the darkness his disciples fled, disappearing like sparks from a dying flame. He who healed and fed and loved, who wept and laughed and shared humanity's lot was no longer alone but was surrounded by violence and contempt.

People: *How vulnerable the heart of God is! How fragile and precious is love, so easily betrayed, so quickly abandoned.*

Leader: O Christ child of God, so long ago angels sang and shepherds worshiped and the heavens echoed with the music of joy and hope. Now you are led shackled through the streets of the city in darkness, abandoned by those you loved. Who can speak the mystery of God's unfathomable mercy?

All: *"Ah, Holy Jesus! . . . Who brought this upon You? It is my treason, Lord, that has undone You. 'Twas I, Lord Jesus, I it was denied You; I crucified You."*[1]

---

1. "Ah, Holy Jesus." Words by Johann Heermann; transl. by Robert Bridges. Reprinted in *Songs, Hymns, & Spiritual Songs* (Louisville: Westminster/John Knox Press, 1990), 93.

Leader: There was no end to the tears. All through the night of bitter emptiness there was no end to the tears.

People: *Jesus' love, his peace, his gentle touch, his healing gaze, his light, God's light, our light: like a candle in a dark wind, it flickered, struggled, went out, and was gone from us.*

Leader: How could we have let this happen? How could we have lost this love that filled us like the dawn fills the eastern sky?

People: *Jesus! Gentle Lord. Kind brother who gathered us around his gentle presence as a good mother gathers in her arms children once lost.*

Leader: There was no end to the weeping. All through the night of sorrow there was no end to the tears.

— silence —

Leader: Jesus said: "Come to me, all you that are weary and are carrying heavy burdens, and I will give you rest."[1] Let the risen Christ give you that rest now.

People: *The Baptist said, "He will baptize you with the Holy Spirit and fire."[2]*

Leader: Let him anoint you now with the Spirit of peace and kindle anew the flame of love in your hearts.

People: *God gave to the beloved Son the most precious gifts in God's creation: God gave you and me to Jesus that we might be his possession, his family, and dwell within his gentle love forever.*

Leader: Nothing has been lost. All shall be restored.

All: *Let us be gathered into the gentleness of Christ, into his love, and into the radiant light of this new day in the kingdom of God. Amen.*

---

1. Matthew 11:28.
2. Matthew 3:11.

⚽ easter season ⚽

Leader: When you enter the land, when you come upon the inheritance of joy, when your heart overflows with grace, and the Spirit, like the waters of the Jordan in flood, flows among you in power and in beauty, when all of this comes upon you in the fullness of time and you enter the sovereignty of God's love, do not forget the one who wandered lost in empty places that you might be found, whose life was broken like a lamb upon the altar that you might be made whole.

People: *Like a lamb upon the altar did our brother die, he who in the wasteland saw the servant glory of all Israel entering the shining walls of Jerusalem and dwelling like a flock among the hills of peace.*

Leader: With a shout we will arise; with a shout we will begin our ascent. Anoint your brother with the oil of gladness. Deck your sister in the garlands of joy. Let each one lead her household forward on our pilgrim march.

People: *For behold, the desert where Jesus was has become a garden. Where darkness dwelt a great light has dawned, and we are led in paths we have not known and in ways beyond our understanding, while before us in the night our God leads like a pillar of fire.*

Leader: For the one who was broken now dances in joy; with the joyous step of victory he dances without restraint. The one who cried out now sings anew the songs of Zion. The one who died outside the walls now leads the minstrels and the pipers through the gates.

People: *Our hearts shall sing forever!*

Leader: Let us go, therefore, into the streets and lanes of the city, even to the highways and the fields, and there speak that gracious word in which we ourselves have tasted peace.

People: *For the one who died on the cross yet lives within us and among us. He has made the night sing and has borne our brokenness and shame. To him we bring both our sorrows and our praises.*

Leader: In love the Savior kneels at sinners' feet.

People: *We have become lamps of Christ's love, a royal family constellated in light and truth, a people who move forward with a shout of joy.*

Leader: No wilderness or desert waste, no shadowy corner of the heart is unknown to God's holy joy.

People: *Let us cast fear, like a worn-out garment, upon the flames of love. Let us come together and move forward, reaching out to others to join us in the gracious company of God's love.*

Leader: And the one who is the resurrection and the life shall with us move into that land where justice, truth, and beauty rise like the very walls of Zion, and generations numberless as the stars go forth in endless song onto the fields of praise; in the name of Jesus. Amen.

litanies for
special occasions

✥ springtime ✥

Leader: Like a song that rises and disappears into a mist of tears; like ice breaking on the river; like the ripping of a bandage; like the green bud dripping with rain; like the sound of distant traffic through open windows on the first warm evening; like the roll of thunder and the flash of ghost lightning as the front moves in; like the music of the chime when the warm wind blows; like a brook high in the mountains fed by melting snow, a brook that becomes a stream, a stream that becomes a river, a river that flows around us and through us; like the river of life that flows through the city of God — so like this is the eternal life that flows to us with each passing moment of the kingdom — eternal beauty, eternal peace, eternal cycles of change and birth and rebirth.

People: *Change can take us by surprise or we can see it coming. Whatever its mode of entrance, we must be gentle and patient with ourselves as we allow the Spirit to weave us into her eternal dance.*

Leader: For behold: the sycamores you gaze upon, the cottonwoods and locusts thick with bud, they are eternal. The sky above their outstretched limbs shall never pass away. And you, O people of God, were created for eternal life.

People: *If we slow ourselves down, if we stop trying to outrace time, we shall discover eternity in each passing moment. If we slow down, we shall be so taken with the eternal beauty around us that we shall be surprised to discover that our resurrection has already taken place.*

Leader: For God dwells among the people. God's home is on earth.

People: *We know in our hearts that Christ already lives among us.*

Leader: New life is breaking forth around us. Within are continually giving birth to our prayers of gratitude and thanksgiving.

People: *We meditate on the ones whom we love and upon those who love us. We stagger under the weight of our countless blessings. We know in our hearts that somewhere, under the same blue sky, our Lord is present with us.*

41

Leader: And now the dance begins — as Love is passed from hand to hand, as the living God makes rounds among the people, and as eternity sculpts us through the great pilgrimage of receiving and letting go that leads finally into the arms of the One whose love never changes. Amen.

❧ for those who have ❧ died in combat

memorial day

Leader: These were not men and women of combat. These were husbands and fathers, sons and daughters, farmers and poets, doctors and teachers, factory workers and longshoremen, carpenters and artists: dreamers, bearers of dreams, defenders of dreams.

People: *Receive them, O Lord, into the eternal peace of your kingdom.*

Leader: These men and women were not created for war. They were created for peace: for the rhythm of the workday and the weekend; for the turning of the seasons and the celebration of holidays; for the gentle play of family and the lasting bonds of friendship. These men and women were not created for war. They were created for peace. Yet they fought with bravery and died with courage.

People: *Receive them, O Lord, into the eternal peace of your kingdom.*

Leader: How long, O Lord, how long? How long must tyranny and oppression, injustice and hatred, require your people to offer living sacrifices on the cruel altar of war? How long must hands created for peace be trained for war? How long must young life be cut short and hearts be broken by the chaos of bloodshed?

People: *Only the one who is peace can bring peace to this troubled world. As those we remember today now dwell in your eternal peace, O Lord, so grant us a measure of that peace in our grieving hearts.*

Leader: The loss we mourn shall not be in vain if, through our brokenness and pain, peace flows forth like a balm for our wounds and for all wounds. And from that pain, from that peace, from that balm, healing shall come upon us and upon this broken world.

All: *Even as healing and peace flowed from the wounds of the one who was broken upon the cross. Amen.*

❧ mother's day ❧

Leader: Like the ocean — vast, turbulent, beautiful — the maternal bears us into life, rocks us gently like waves against a shore, lifts us up and lowers us down, whispers, caresses, strokes with eternal tenderness. The mirror for our first smile is our mother's smile, and the occasion for our first laughter is our mother's laughter.

People: *A mother's love for her child is deep, like the veined ores of the earth. It is as powerful and fierce as spring bursting the bonds of winter. Her loyalty is as pure as silver refined seven-fold.*

Leader: Our mothers brought us forth in pain and joy. They nurtured, taught, disciplined, and watched over us while we were young. They fretted and rejoiced over us as we grew and matured. Their care and love extends our whole lives.

People: *Who would sing the joy and the heartache of motherhood, the height and depth of its fierce and powerful love? The mother rejoices when the child rejoices, suffers when the child suffers.*

Leader: O God, in motherhood you have given us a model of your steadfast love, a love that never lets us go, that never gives up, that abides with us all the days of our lives.

People: *We honor our mothers, who had no manual for the job of raising us. We honor them in their imperfection and in their courage. We honor them in their strength and in their power. As sons and daughters, we cherish and love them for every act of kindness and caring they have given to us.*

Leader: A mother's love is as ancient as time, steadfast as the stars, fierce as spring, strong as iron, powerful as the ocean, gentle as a whisper, tender as her child. O God, bless our mothers and mothers everywhere for their courage and faith in undertaking the lifelong challenge of motherhood; in Jesus' name. Amen.

❧ father's day ❧

Leader: Fatherhood is a mystery like the mountains, or the forest, or the timeless cycle of the seasons changing and turning and returning again: the heavens nourishing with rain, the towering clouds chastising with thunder, the gentle touch of snow falling silently, the wealth of summer pulsing with life and heat. Our fathers tower above us, and their fathers before them, and their fathers before them.

People: *Down through the generations, from father to son, from father to daughter, the wisdom of fatherhood is imparted.*

Leader: Strong yet gentle, ready to defend yet marked with vulnerability, humbled by the mystery of their role yet ready to teach because young eyes look up to them, our fathers are men who impart to us an example for life.

Daughters: *We know our fathers' tenderness, their charm, their limitations, and their vulnerability. Our fathers are only human, and we honor them as they have honored the challenge of parenting.*

Sons: *By their example, our fathers taught us about ourselves. Student and teacher thrown together by the mystery of destiny, we learned from our fathers in many ways: by what they taught and didn't teach, by what they did and didn't do. Our fathers are only human, and we honor them as they have honored the challenge of parenting.*

Leader: O God, our knowledge of you is shaped and formed by those who care for us and guide us as we grow to maturity. Today we honor our fathers and the role of fatherhood, for the men who have guided us have led us to the knowledge of your love, your strength, your eternal caring.

All: *Let us rejoice in the gift of our fathers and of their fathers before them. Let us honor the men who would take on the great responsibility of fatherhood. Let us give thanks for the fathering we have received and for the mystery of fatherhood, which like the mountains and the forest, towers above us with the shadows of love. Amen.*

45

the fourth of july

Leader: To the land of the Shawnee and the Iroquois, of the Arapaho and the Cheyenne, we have come from every corner of the globe: from the blazing plains of Africa and the frozen fjords of Norway; from the wheat fields of the Ukraine and the rice paddies of Asia; from South America and India and the Middle East; from Europe and Australia and the scattered islands of the Pacific.

People: *We are different colors, different faiths, different cultures, yet as one people under God we celebrate and commemorate freedom's birth.*

Leader: Our founding fathers had a vision for the new nation for which they had fought, yet how wondrously greater is the reality of our land today than even the dream of the first patriots!

People: *The price of freedom is not cheap. From Bunker Hill to Shiloh and from Gettysburg to Montgomery, Alabama, the people have had to continually work at ensuring and protecting freedom for all Americans.*

Leader: As ancient Israel followed God's pillar of fire out of slavery, so too we must rededicate ourselves today to follow that same blazing light toward a new birth of freedom and justice.

People: *Amen.*

Leader: We must not rest in our work or in our vigilance. We must ascend to the mountaintop to behold the fullness of the dream sown by Jefferson and Madison, by Lincoln and King.

People: *Amen.*

Leader: For the gift of freedom is both a trust and a risk. In this promised land we must learn to use our freedom wisely, to choose carefully, to act responsibly.

People: *O God of freedom, you have blessed our land and watched over us. Inspire us by your Spirit to rejoice in the gift of freedom, to use our freedom wisely, and to ever strive for freedom and justice to rain down upon all our people.*

Leader: And we shall be like a new Israel, a tapestry of colors and cultures and faiths as rich as Joseph's coat of many colors, whirling and flashing in the winds of freedom, cleansed in the waters of justice, shining in the light of liberty.

All: *Amen.*

❧ harvest time ❧

Leader: The leaves of the cottonwood have turned yellow, the maple red. The skies are filled with flocks of birds heading south. Young people leave for college, children for school. Yellow buses ply the back roads between harvest fields. In the morning the air is cool and clear, the sky so blue it might have been created new while we slept. All of nature is dying, a peaceful, glorious death, a transfiguration of loveliness and melancholy. All is eternally changing, turning, being made new, being reborn, and we must cast fear aside to prepare for the releasing and receiving that the dawning kingdom of God is bringing upon us.

People: *Perfect love casts out fear.*[1] *Perfect love loosens our grasping hands that we might be free to accept God's honors as a gift. Perfect love liberates us to feel our feelings, think our thoughts, respect and honor ourselves and others.*

Leader: We must not be afraid to allow sorrow to have its way with us. Change brings grief, letting go, loss. But God gently relieves us of one circumstance only to give us, as a gift, something even more beautiful, even more precious.

People: *As we enter the eternity of the kingdom, let us not be afraid to weep long and hard, both in joy for what is now ours and in sorrow and relief for what we and God have endured to win this bright victory.*

Leader: For tears purify the soul. They cleanse the heart. Like the rain, they water the earth and leave the air fresh and clear. Tears guide us toward joy, toward laughter, toward the dancing and feasting of the wedding banquet.

People: *Who are we, that we should be invited to sit at the table in the kingdom with our Lord?*

Leader: You are children of God, sons and daughters of the Most High, the new Israel of God, the good wheat planted so long ago, disciples to the One from Nazareth, fellow bearers of his cross.

---

1. 1 John 4:18.

48

People: *If these words are true, then we must love and honor ourselves and others with a passion and caring we have not known before. We must open our hearts to feelings and thoughts as broad and sweeping and deep as God's kingdom itself.*

Leader: For fear is passing away and Love has made her entrance, and Christ moves among the people in patience and strength, waiting for the day when our steps shall carry us to his door. Amen.

❧ thanksgiving (or any) day ❧

Leader: Sin offerings will one day come to an end. Sacrifices for atonement will cease. But thank offerings will never come to an end. Thanksgiving shall rise from the people of God in one endless, eternal song, filling all of earth and all of heaven with a hymn of gratitude that shall never fall silent.

People: *O God, we have so much to be thankful for! So many big things, so many little things. Our hearts overflow with thanksgiving. Our cup runneth over, and our tongues are not adequate to express the depth of our joy and gratitude.*

Leader: O people, let the Spirit take the song of thanksgiving in your heart, inarticulate with joy, and lift it up before God. In silence let us meditate on the blessings that have been poured forth upon us.

— silence —

Leader: O God, you are closer to us than we are to our very selves. You are the ground of our being and of every prayer we utter. Even when we cannot find words, you understand, you hear us, you fathom our hearts.

People: *The blessings that are ours — they are beyond number. The thanksgiving in our hearts — who could find words for it? The joy that sustains us — who could give it adequate expression? Our hearts dance and sing and shout, all at the same time.*

Leader: O people, hear the word of your God: "Those who bring thanksgiving as their sacrifice honor me; to those who go the right way I will show the salvation of God."[1] Amen.

---

1. Psalm 50:23.

50

litanies for
the seasons of the heart

❧ thanksgiving ❧

Leader: Thanksgiving has no altar other than the human heart, no temple stronger than the tabernacle of clasped hands, no chalice more sacred than the kiss offered with a smile, no music more holy than tears, no dance more jubilant than laughter, no chant more gracious than the infant's wail, no ceremony more precious than the courtship of love, no offering more holy than outstretched arms to hold one who is wounded.

People: *We are overwhelmed by the grace that has come upon us! We will give thanks in silence.*

— silence —

Leader: Healing, friendship, love, family, children, shelter, food, clothing.

People: *Color, trees, animals, the stars, strength, safety, meaning, freedom, life: How alike we are to one another in our neediness! How unified we become in our gratitude! What a harmony of love does thanksgiving reign down upon the household of God!*

— silence —

Leader: Behold the family of God! What is yours today can never be taken from you. Go forth, therefore, unafraid to let your heart reveal its wounds of tenderness. Let your tears of sorrow and joy soak the fabric of your strong embrace. Let your laughter unleash a dance that will never end. Set ablaze the kindled passion of your undared dreams.

All: *For God's joy is our joy; God's strength is our strength; and God's thanksgiving is our thanksgiving. Amen.*

༄ a time of loss ༅

Leader: "A generation goes, and a generation comes, but the earth remains forever. The sun rises and the sun goes down, and hurries to the place where it rises. . . . All streams run to the sea, but the sea is not full; to the place where the streams flow, there they continue to flow."[1]

People: *The gift of life is a mystery greater than we can comprehend. It is full of joy and celebration.*

Leader: It is woven with sorrow and regret.

People: *It is blessed with pleasure and delight.*

Leader: It is touched by pain and grief.

People: *We receive it as a gift unasked for. We let go of it as a precious treasure beyond value.*

Leader: For everything there is a season, and a time for every matter under heaven: a time to be born, and a time to die;

People: *A time to plant, and a time to pluck up what is planted;*

Leader: A time to mourn and time to dance;

People: *A time to weep and a time to laugh.*[2]

Leader: Even the tallest cottonwood by the riverbank must fall some day. Even the most ancient oak must someday return to the soil from which it grew.

People: *O Lord, in our loss we are consoled by your promise of eternal life. In our grief we are strengthened by precious memories of laughter shared, of work accomplished, of a life fully lived. Our sorrow is tempered with the joy of having shared in the life we celebrate today.*

Leader: "All people are grass, their constancy is like the flower of the field. The grass withers, the flower fades, when the breath of the

---

1. Ecclesiastes 1:4–5,7.
2. Ecclesiastes 3:1–4, paraphrased.

LORD blows upon it; surely the people are grass. The grass withers, the flower fades; but the word of our God will stand forever.[3]

All: *The one who came from on high seeking the lost, healing the sick, and offering his life said: "I am the resurrection and the life. Do not let your hearts be troubled. . . . In my Father's house there are many dwelling places. Whoever believes in the Son has eternal life."*[4] Amen.

---

3. Isaiah 40:6–8.
4. John 11:25; 14:1–2; 3:36.

↤ a time of grieving ↦

Leader: Comfort, O comfort my people, says your God.[1] Speak tenderly to my children, and tell them their sorrow, their brokenness, is known in heaven, is known to my heart.

People: *The pain, the loss, the anger. It is difficult to speak.*

Leader: The Spirit carries our hearts, torn with grief, into that light we find so difficult to see at this moment. The Spirit speaks when we cannot. The Spirit prays when we are too numb to pray. The Spirit utters the depth of our sorrow when we are too choked with grief to whisper the word that might console.

People: *The one who has formed us into a household of faith was a man of sorrows acquainted with grief. He came from the radiance of heaven and knew the realm of shadows we taste in this moment.*

Leader: Blessed are those who mourn, for they will be comforted.[2] Martha said quietly to her sister, "The Teacher is here, and is calling for you."[3] Mary ran to him and fell at his feet, weeping. He was greatly disturbed in spirit and deeply moved. Jesus began to weep.[4]

— silence —

Leader: The tears of God's children are like the gentle rains of spring. They soften the earth; they warm the rivers and the seas; they bring forth new life.

People: *O Lord, speak gently to us and abide with us in our loss. In your good time let healing come to our wounded hearts; let goodness and joy arise from the ashes of our grief. Grant us strength to bear what at times seems unbearable.*

Leader: Innocence and love entered the world from on high only to be broken on the cross. The one who healed and taught was not

---

1. Isaiah 40:1.
2. Matthew 5:4.
3. John 11:28.
4. John 11:35.

56

defeated by grief or death, but rose into newness of life, transforming sorrow into joy, violence into peace.

All: *We offer our grieving, wounded hearts to you, O God. Transform them, heal them, that our souls may yet sing again in thanksgiving for the mystery of receiving and letting go that is life. Amen.*

≈ national tragedy ≈

Leader: From the ice-bound peaks of the Cascades to the heat-soaked shores of the Gulf, from the Appalachians to the Rockies, in small towns with church steeples rising in the morning sun, in gleaming cities with skylines reaching toward the heavens, at every crossroads village and every seaport town, the shadow of the angel of death has wounded the hearts of our people all across this good land.

People: *We gather this morning shaken by what has come upon our nation. Our grief is deep. Our need for God's reassuring love is great.*

Leader: The one who shattered the bonds of death and rose in power and glory says to you: "Do not be afraid. Remember, I am with you always, to the end of the age."[1]

People: *Now we know the depth of our need for you, O Lord. Now we know how vulnerable we are, how fragile and precious are life and peace.*

Leader: O Lord, cradle your people in your strong arms that we might weep away the sorrow in our hearts. Strengthen us by your Spirit and lead us through this valley of grief toward the light of healing and resurrection.

People: *May our tears soak the soil of our beloved country like spring rain. And like the gentle rains of spring, may they bring as their harvest a new sense of gratitude for the blessings that are ours; a new birth of kindness and compassion among our people.*

Leader: For God watches over us. God abides with us in our sorrow. "I will be with you in trouble. I will answer when you call,"[2] says the Lord.

People: *We stand in such need of you, Lord, and so in need of prayer.*

Leader: O people, deep within the hidden chamber of your hearts the one who is the way and the truth and the resurrection and the life whispers to you: "Do not be afraid. I am with you always." Amen.

---

1. Matthew 14:27; 28:20.
2. Psalm 91:15, paraphrased.

ঙ national blessing ঙ

Leader: Silver and gold, grain and wheat, weapons and armies, power and influence — these things our nation has in abundance. Our cities of steel and glass rise toward the heavens, and our small towns and villages dot a landscape that has known peace within its borders for over 130 years. Yet does not the cry for justice, the cry for freedom, the cry for equality, still ring out in our land?

People: *The nation that stands under God's blessing stands also under God's judgment. God judges a nation not by its wealth and power, but by the quality of mercy and justice that is found among its people.*

Leader: In the shadow of the skyscraper the crumbling ghetto spreads its ruthless asphalt. On the hills and plains of the countryside the family farm must be sold and abandoned. Too often the weak and vulnerable are blamed for their misfortune instead of assisted. And in too many hearts the hidden hatred of racism poisons the fabric of our communities.

People: *O God, you have blessed our land with prosperity, with peace, and with power. It is not for these that we petition you this morning, but rather for a new spiritual birth among our people.*

Leader: O God, instill anew in the hearts of our people a thirst for justice, a love of equality, a readiness for tolerance, a willingness to confront the darkness within our own hearts that compassion might flow instead of judgment and hatred.

People: *Bless our land, O God, with a new gratitude for the great blessings that are ours, and fill us with the longing to see all Americans share in the goodness of justice, equality, and prosperity.*

Leader: Bless us, O God, with a new zeal to bind up the fabric of our communities torn by mistrust, prejudice, and intolerance.

People: *Bless our land, O God, with a new birth of love among our people. Then we will rejoice and give thanks, because we will have pleased you, the one who loves justice and mercy more than power and wealth.*

Leader: And then not just peace, but true *shalom* shall dwell among our people. We shall be one people with many differences, united in the justice, the equality, and the tolerance we have given to one another through God's Spirit. Amen.

꩜ humility ꩜

Leader: Considering themselves righteous and holy, convinced they knew the mind and opinions of God, sure they had in their holy book the truth of eternal life — these were the men who handed the Lord of life over to be crucified.

People: *Jesus said to them: "You search the scriptures because you think that in them you have eternal life.... Yet you refuse to come to me to have life."*[1]

Leader: People of God, it is not a book we worship, but the living God; not words on paper, but the risen Christ, alive, moving among us, breathing his Spirit into our hearts.

People: *And where the risen Christ is present, there love, compassion, acceptance, and tolerance flow like new wine.*

Leader: The Scriptures and the Gospel stories must lead us to the feet of the risen Christ, with whom we must walk in humility and love as servants in the world, condemning hatred, intolerance, oppression, and violence, but also practicing his words: "Do not judge, so that you may not be judged."[2]

People: *O Lord, guard us from the sin of self-righteousness and presumption lest we become blind and arrogant like those who condemned you. Remind us that our knowledge is partial, that we are not gods, but only humans, and that only you can judge another's worthiness for eternal life. Amen.*

---

1. John 5:39–40.
2. Matthew 7:1.

❧ for youth ❧

Leader: Like an army of hope, like a legion of promise, like a harvest of new dreams, so the younger generation rises to meet the challenge of the world, takes upon its youthful shoulders the yoke of history, embraces the task of carrying forward the work and the joy of living.

People: *The poetry of the generations sings of knowledge handed down, of wisdom passed on, of responsibilities shifted, of youthful hands and minds and hearts boldly reaching out to receive the burden and the delight of charting the human destiny.*

Leader: Let us admire our young people in their courage, in their exuberance and energy. Let us applaud them for both their earnestness and their playfulness. Let us delight in their seeking and in their finding. Let us take pleasure in their beauty and strength.

People: *They are like young saplings in the house of God, green and full of life.*

Leader: Let us give our young people the trust and respect they deserve. As life has honored us, so let us honor them as inheritors and trustees of the creation we have enjoyed.

People: *Each generation steps into a world it did not shape. Each generation is given blessings and challenges unique to its destiny. Help us, O God, to equip and guide our young people as they undertake the work of your kingdom.*

Leader: When they seek you, Lord, may they find you as we have.

People: *For you have been our dwelling place in all generations.*[1]

Leader: And when that day comes for us to enter upon eternity, we shall leave this beautiful world knowing that, in the hands of our sons and daughters, it will be as it was in the beginning, as it is now and ever shall be — world without end. Amen.

---

1. Psalm 90:1.

❧ restored relationships ❧

Leader: The covenant broken, the weeping people are driven into exile. The prodigal takes the inheritance and leaves home, and the father's step is heavy with sorrow. The nails are driven and the cross raised, and the Light is extinguished.

— silence —

Leader: But God restores the people. They return to Zion singing and dancing. The prodigal comes home, and the father runs in joy to greet him, arms outstretched in love. And on the evening of the third day, the one who died abandoned and alone returns in peace and mercy.

People: *The movement of God's Spirit is to restore what is broken, to heal what has been torn, to recreate what has been destroyed.*

Leader: O God, each of us has known the pain of broken relationships. We have breached the bond with ourselves, you, a family member, a loved one, a friend, or an institution. Too often our lives are littered with burned bridges.

People: *Yet our Christ calls us continually toward healing, toward reaching out to mend what has been broken, toward reconciling what has been torn asunder.*

Leader: Hear, therefore, O God, the prayers of your people: for marriages torn by mistrust but healed by your love

People: *We pray and give thanks.*

Leader: For friendships lost through betrayal and resentment but recreated and rediscovered through your Spirit

People: *We pray and give thanks.*

Leader: For the bonds between parent and child strained and conflicted yet reconciled by your grace

People: *We pray and give thanks.*

Leader: For respect and gentleness in the wake of divorce

People: *We pray and give thanks.*

Leader: For families torn by strife yet reconciled in the light of Christ's love

People: *We pray and give thanks.*

Leader: For whole peoples torn by the divisions of race or religion or culture yet working to find common ground on which to live in harmony

People: *We pray and give thanks.*

Leader: O God, the one who was broken that we might be restored, lead us on toward one great reconciliation, one great healing. Keep us ever at the ready to mend our torn relationships and sustain us in the hope that all that has been broken in our lives, all that has been lost, all that has been torn apart will one day, in your good time, be restored and healed; in Jesus' name. Amen.

~ acceptance and grace ~

Leader: The thirsty earth asks not for the rains of spring, but they come. The birds return unbidden, and the flowers emerge unasked for. The days of summer, radiant with heat and light, fragrant with growth and life, unfold one by one. The winds of autumn polish the sky, and the trees cast their royal garments to the ground. The silence of winter descends like the purity of the stars. The seasons come and go, life bursts forth and then recedes, the wheel of life turns: all of this is ours unrequested; all of this beauty and wealth is unearned, unmerited.

People: *If we could grasp what a gift life is in itself: the simple miracles of breath, of sight, of touch, of sound, of smell; if we could fathom the wealth that is ours without a single demand, a single petition, a single act of obedience or service, perhaps we could begin to understand a love so great that it asks nothing in return but love itself.*

Leader: The agenda of Love is love. The response to love is acceptance. The proper return for generosity is receiving.

People: *Yet we feel more comfortable when we can earn a reward, as if we could control matters better if there were an equal exchange*

Leader: Gaze upon the heavens, people, and consider the mighty oceans. Look to the winds that bring the clouds and to the rivers that water the land. Observe the stars wheeling in their courses and the mighty forests rising in the towering mountains. What is there here of equality? What is there here that you can repay, that you can merit? Behold the Son of God nailed to a cross for you. How could you ever earn such love, such grace?

People: *O God, so often we rush about the world trying to justify our lives with deeds, trying to merit the gift of your love through our accomplishments, through what we think is obedience.*

Leader: Help us to understand that your love would gently arrest us in our anxious attempts to earn your acceptance, would quietly lead us aside to still waters and green pastures, there to find the peace you have already won for us, already prepared for us, and for which we need do nothing but accept and rejoice.

People: *The one who knelt at sinners' feet taught that we must become as children to enter his kingdom. Our hands must be open to receive.*

Leader: We cannot earn, we cannot merit, we cannot manipulate a love that is offered as freely as the rains water the spring earth, as freely as the breath of summer rustles the green leaves of the cottonwood.

People: *To receive, to accept, to trust that God's grace and love cannot be thwarted, cannot be defeated, not even by ourselves — this is the work of our faith.*

Leader: Help us, O Lord, to humbly accept the gift of your love, that we may grasp the depth and height by which we are accepted by you; in the name of Jesus. Amen.

❧ courage and strength ❧

Leader: Courage is not the absence of fear, but the capacity to act in the presence of fear. Faith is not the absence of doubt, but the courage to believe in spite of doubt. Trust is not the absence of qualms, but the capacity to go forward despite misgivings.

People: *We thought we were brave. We thought we were strong.*

Leader: But we had not expected what has come upon us.

People: *We thought ourselves prepared, ready, but now we discover that we are trembling. What looms before us is unknown, full of risk, menacing.*

Leader: Listen to the word of your God, people: "Fear not, my people, my beloved children. I have heard your cries. I have measured the depth of your fear. I stand with you before the unknown future you face. Fear not! Cast your troubles and fears upon my heart. For I am a mighty God, able to bear you home even as a shepherd bears the sheep home to the fold."

People: *God dwells more closely with us than we do to our very selves. We move and have our being in God, who walks with us step by step through every danger and every threat.*

Leader: The one who is the resurrection and life said: "Ask, and it will be given you; search, and you will find; knock, and the door will be opened for you."[1]

People: *Never before have we stood in such need of you, O God. Never before have we stood so in need of prayer.*

Leader: O God, let your Holy Spirit guide us deep into ourselves where you dwell, where strength and courage well up and flow, where we shall discover the imperishable and unconquerable love in which we are held eternally, where we shall find peace in the midst of the threats before us.

---

1. Matthew 7:7.

People: *And we shall go forward with courage and strength, secure in the knowledge that the one who died for each of us will never let us go.*

Leader: God will never lose us.

People: *God will abide with us to the end.*

All: *The Lord will receive us finally into the eternal glory of the Father's kingdom. Amen.*

✢ reconciliation ✢

Leader: Deeds have been done. Action taken. Words have been spoken. The seeds of suspicion and mistrust have been sown, and our harvest is bitter indeed. Where once was openness, now walls have been erected. Where once the hand of fellowship was easy to extend, now it seems almost impossible. Where once there was unity, now division prevails.

People: *What have we become, and what are we becoming? We thought we knew about love and forgiveness, about tolerance and acceptance. Why then does resentment run so deep in us? Why are we so torn by strife? Why does peace seem so far from us?*

Leader: The men Jesus called to follow him were natural enemies: Simon and Andrew, impoverished fishermen; James and John from the wealthier class; and Matthew, the tax gatherer, the enemy of both. The lesson Jesus would teach them was not easy or cheap. It would cost him his life.

People: *The disciples thought they knew themselves, only to abandon Jesus in the end. We thought we knew ourselves, but now we find that the strife that tears us apart is too great for us.*

Leader: The ground on which we are gathered is consecrated by the blood of the one who came to heal and to save. He has called us together not because we are all the same or because we agree on everything, but rather that we might learn the hard lessons of love, lessons that are forged in the crucible of difference and disagreement.

People: *O Lord, we stand in need of prayer. We stand in need of you. We stand in need of a new birth of love and tolerance among us.*

Leader: In our differences, in our strife, we must search for common ground on which to begin to rebuild our community of trust and love. We will find that common ground beneath the shadow of Jesus' cross, on which all the violence and conflict of humanity was reconciled in the one who was broken for each of us.

People: *O Lord, untie the knots of bitterness and resentment that bind our hearts. Help us to set aside our wounded pride, mindful of the wounds you bore for our sake. Gently grant us the courage to take the first step toward reconciliation, to be the first to reach out, to begin the healing.*

Leader: Love is patient; love is kind; love is not envious or boastful or arrogant or rude. It does not insist on its own way; it is not irritable or resentful; it does not rejoice in wrongdoing, but rejoices in the truth. It bears all things, believes all things, hopes all things, endures all things.[1] Amen.

---

1. 1 Corinthians 13:4–7.

❧ friendship ❧

Leader: Ruth and Naomi, King David and Jonathan, God and Abraham: the great friendships of Scripture testify to steadfast love, to the mutual delight of kindred spirits, to loyalty tested by time, to fidelity forged in circumstances both harsh and pleasant.

People: *The door of friendship swings open unexpectedly. Spontaneous and surprising, like spring emerging after a long winter we thought would never end, true friendship is a pure gift from on high.*

Leader: Friendship liberates us to be who we are. Friendship frees us to grow and change, to explore ourselves and life, to become what God intended us to be.

People: *Our friends sustain us and stand by us as we discover ourselves. They nurture and encourage our growth. They rejoice in our discoveries and in our evolving self-understanding.*

Leader: Friendship is the soil from which all love emerges. Friendship is the bedrock of the life companionship we call marriage.

People: *True friendship is delightful because it respects our integrity. It does not try to own us. It does not try to manipulate us. It does not seek to change us.*

Leader: Friendship is the equation in which God's gift of freedom finds its highest expression. To our friends we freely give our affection, our loyalty, and our support, which in turn we receive without charge from them.

People: *O God, how delightful is friendship, how precious are our friends! Teach us to treasure and nurture the friendships you have given us, and let us be always open to the surprise of new friendship.*

Leader: On the night before his death, the Christ said to his disciples: "You are my friends if you do what I command you. I do not call you servants any longer, because the servant does not know what the master is doing; but I have called you friends, because I have made known to you everything that I have heard from my Father."[1]

People: *Lord, of the many gifts of friendship you have given us, keep us mindful that the gift of your friendship is the greatest of all, from which all graces and all good things flow. Amen.*

---

1. John 15:14–15.

❧ for the family ❧

Leader: Wherever acceptance is extended no matter what; wherever tolerance and love, compassion and respect flow steadily no matter where we have been or what we have done; wherever we are always welcome; wherever the door always opens at our knock — there is family, there is home, there is the household of God to which we truly belong.

People: *Parents and children, brothers and sisters, uncles and aunts, grandparents and friends — our families, no matter what their form, are a precious gift from God, a sanctuary where we can find rest and peace in an indifferent world.*

Leader: In the sanctuary of the family we are appreciated for our uniqueness, for who we are and not what we do.

People: *In the sanctuary of the family we can find support and healing from a world that often batters and wounds our souls.*

Leader: The family is a crucible wherein the gospel can take form and be forged.

People: *If the gospel is to live anywhere in this broken world, it must live within our families. If the gospel is to be learned and practiced, it must blossom among those to whom we are closest.*

Leader: In the crucible of the family, in the intimate dynamics of family life, there the gospel truths — tolerance, acceptance, love, forgiveness — there they must be practiced, precisely where it is most necessary and most difficult.

People: *The family is a classroom where priceless lessons are taught and examples set.*

Leader: In the classroom of the family, the Scriptures live and the Spirit teaches. In the classroom of the family, values are passed on from one generation to the next.

People: *In the classroom of the family, the gospel story is handed down that the children of our children shall know the Good News of God's abiding love.*

Leader: Sanctuary, crucible, classroom — our families, like all God's blessings, are both a gift and a challenge. Within the family the seed of the kingdom is planted and nurtured. Within the family unconditional love must grow and mature, becoming a mirror of God's steadfast and unwavering acceptance of each of us.

People: *O God, help us to forge the sanctuaries of our families into havens of love that they may become an oasis not only where we might find peace, healing, and love, but where your gentle presence might abide and find the love for which you created us; in the name of Jesus. Amen.*

❧ forgiveness ❧

Leader: If we could grasp the height and depth of the love with which we are loved, the passionate tenderness with which our souls are watched over, the eternal gentleness by which we are shepherded through life, we would never come into the presence of the Most High without a song on our lips and a dance in our hearts.

People: *For we were created for love, shaped and destined by the Creator's hand before the beginning of time for life's full cup of gladness and challenge and for heaven's bright domain.*

Leader: Yet we are flawed and incomplete creatures. We make mistakes. We fail ourselves and others. We injure those we love and betray our own deepest selves.

People: *O God, our inadequacy keeps us from experiencing your love. Too often we prevent ourselves from knowing your forgiveness because we cannot forgive ourselves. Too often we blind ourselves to your love because we cannot forgive others.*

Leader: God's mercy, God's forgiveness are ours even before we ask. God's love pours down upon us eternally, patiently awaiting our awakening to its truth.

People: *Let us untie the knots of bitterness and resentment that bind our hearts. Let us be gentle with ourselves and prepare our souls to receive the one who came not to judge but to save by letting forgiveness flow from our hearts to those we resent.*

Leader: O Lord, by the grace of your Holy Spirit, let the gentleness of your love unclench the hearts of your people, flooding their souls with love and mercy that they may come before you with a song on their lips and a dance in their hearts. Amen.

❧ christian unity ❧

Leader: First Jesus called the poor, Simon and Andrew, fishermen with only their nets. Then he called the wealthy, James and John, who climbed down out of their boat to follow him. Then he called the enemy of both, Levi the tax collector. So it is that Christ's love calls into fellowship those who would normally be set against one another.

People: *One person reads the Scriptures one way, and another person reads them differently. One person holds this opinion, and another holds to something contrary. One person sees the Christ in a particular light while another views him through different eyes. For one person the church doors are wide; for another they are narrow.*

Leader: Like the first followers, like the disciples themselves, we are a community of unique individuals with differing experiences, differing backgrounds, and differing views. Yet we are called together into the mystery of the one God and into the fellowship of the one who taught forgiveness, even unto death on the cross.

People: *Would that we could stand on the stony path to Golgotha and witness the passage of him who came from on high to teach the way of love! Truly, could we perceive the suffering humility of love, our proud opinions, our arrogant judgments, our rancorous divisions would surely melt away and evaporate.*

Leader: For love such as the Christ taught does not divide. It unites. It heals. It unifies. It humbles.

People: *O Lord, help us to look ever more carefully into our own hearts to see the self-righteousness and arrogant opinion that dwells there. Teach us that love, not right opinion, is the proper measure of our fidelity to you.*

Leader: Interpretations will always differ. Opinions will always vary. Viewpoints will always be diverse. But God's love will abide. Charity will bind us together in unity in the midst of our diversity.

People: *We will not all think the same. We will not all believe the same. We will not all interpret the same. We will not always agree. But we will all love the same, bearing with one another in mutual honor and respect, patiently accepting those who are different, that the world may know we are Christians by our love; in Jesus' name. Amen.*

❧ renewal ❧

Leader: The barren cottonwood waits patiently and silently through the dark days of winter. Without murmur or complaint it waits quietly for spring's bright clarion to blow. Beneath snow and ice, the dreaming earth waits to be born anew. The rivers run to the sea. The sea gives birth to the clouds, which pour their rain upon the mountains, where the water gathers to the rivers, which run to the sea again. The lion and the elk alike await their food from God's hand, and beneath the soil the seedling of the crocus and the tulip wait to break forth into sunlight. All creation is being born and reborn, created and re-created, eternally moving from life to death to newness of life, eternally waiting for God's breath to bring new life.

People: *The one who is the resurrection and the life calls us to newness of life, invites us to share in the transfiguration of rebirth and renewal.*

Leader: For he said: "No one who puts a hand to the plow and looks back is fit for the kingdom of God."[1] The Savior calls us ever forward into what is new, away from our old, broken self and into the rebirth of our new being in Christ.

People: *To be born anew is the work of the Spirit. We must be like the leafless cottonwood or the dreaming earth in winter or the seedling of the crocus and tulip, waiting patiently, in stillness and silence, for God's Spirit to move upon us.*

Leader: For those who wait upon the LORD shall renew their strength, they shall mount up with wings like eagles, they shall run and not be weary, they shall walk and not faint.[2]

People: *O Lord, we wait upon your Spirit and in our waiting look within to the gospel seed you have planted.*

Leader: We long to break forth and blossom into new being.

---

1. Luke 9:62.
2. Isaiah 40:31.

People: *If what you have sown, Lord, is choked with cares and anxieties, with the distractions and allures of the world, then gently clear a space for us to be born anew and grow.*

Leader: For as the Sower is eternally patient with us, so we must be patient with ourselves and with the work of the Spirit. As the mother must wait nine months for her time to come, so we must wait patiently for the work of rebirth to be accomplished within us.

People: *And as the winter turns to spring, and spring unfolds to summer, and summer leads to the harvest time, so we, in God's good time, shall come to newness of life, continually reborn from the old and into the new, following the one who is the resurrection and the life into the kingdom and into the inheritance of eternal life; in Jesus' name. Amen.*

❧ healing and wholeness ❧

Leader: The one who was whole came into the world only to be broken by the world. The one who brought healing to the world walked our dusty roads only to be wounded and torn. The one who brought peace amid strife, who lifted up what was cast down and made whole what was broken, ended his life broken and cast away.

People: *In the one on the cross we behold our own brokenness and the world's brokenness. There we see the agony of God's suffering love on behalf of the world. This love held nothing back. It was an offering without measure or boundary.*

Leader: If we live long enough in this world, we too come to share in its brokenness. We also are wounded. We also are torn. Yet our healing begins when we recognize the solidarity of the Broken One with us in our suffering.

People: *The disciples were huddled behind locked doors that night when Jesus came to them. They had not believed the women, and they were torn apart by fear and self-hatred.*

Leader: Yet when he came to them, the risen one brought them peace, and with peace, wholeness, and with wholeness, healing, and with healing, strength. He brought not judgment, not condemnation, but wholeness, healing.

People: *O Lord, we wait for you as the disciples did on the evening of the third day. Deep within us there are wounds we cannot heal alone. We are broken inside in ways we cannot even name.*

Leader: Yet the one who sees the secret chamber of our hearts knows our need. He took our humanity on himself and knows its frailties and vulnerability. The risen one brings with him the cup of healing and the balm of wholeness.

People: *O Lord, our Lord, give us your cup of healing that we may drink of it. Anoint us with your balm of peace that we may be glad.*

Leader: Stand before us, O Lord, that we may behold in the wholeness of your risen presence our own wholeness.

People: *Come to us that we may experience in the light of resurrection our own healing; that we may perceive in the joy of your countenance the purity that is within us. Amen.*

✎ for persons with mental illness ✎

Leader: The one who healed all who came to him said, "You shall love the Lord your God with all your heart, and with all your soul, and with all your mind."[1] But what are we to do when the mind is broken, when the delicate chemistry of the brain has gone awry, when the precious self we knew and loved has been shattered and torn at the core of its being?

People: *With deeds of great power the Christ cast out demons, healing those whose minds were sick and tormented. With compassion and mercy he ministered to the demon plagued Gerasene and left him restored to his right mind, dressed in his own clothes, and sitting quietly at Jesus' feet.*

Leader: Today the healing ministry of Christ to persons with mental illness is spread among myriad hands: dedicated doctors and scientists, nurses, case workers, family members, and the people of God, who are called to create a haven and sanctuary for those struggling with brain disorders by sharing the good news of God's healing power where it can be heard and believed.

People: *The fear and stigma of mental illness have no place in God's house. Here we know there is no brokenness, no wound, no illness beyond the healing power of Christ's bright light.*

Leader: We must open our hearts to persons with mental illness and to their families. We must not allow them to become isolated in their suffering. The household of God must be a safe space where the mind, so beautiful, so fragile, can find the peace and welcoming embrace necessary for healing.

People: *O God, we lift up to you all those who experience mental illness. We lift up their families and all those who work for their healing. Guide us by your Spirit that we too may become agents of healing against these terrible diseases, that we may carry on the work of our Lord in healing broken minds; in Jesus' name. Amen.*

---

1. Matthew 22:37.

commitment to the lonely

Leader: Food, television, alcohol, drugs, money, possessions — such are the idols to which the lonely lift up their souls, seeking a balm for that empty space within that only God can fill. Their hope is a vain hope, and their search a vain search, for only the living God can fill the emptiness that lies at the heart of loneliness.

People: *Only the one who knew the loneliness of the cross, who knew utter abandonment, who tasted loneliness for us all can truly touch the deepest point of our isolation.*

Leader: Even we who are known to God, who come together to seek God's presence, know loneliness. We may know it today. The person next to us in the pew may be dying silently from loneliness, from isolation.

People: *The pain of isolation is a deep pain. It is a searing wound to the soul.*

Leader: Loneliness is an invisible predator that stalks our culture. It is a silent plague that afflicts everyone, and yet few acknowledge it or speak of it. It is at the heart of our creaturely condition and therefore at the core of our need for salvation.

People: *O God, there is such solidarity among us in our neediness, if we were but honest with each other! Behind the outer mask we show the world, we stand as lonely, needy creatures in desperate search of love and community.*

Leader: Let the walls of false pride fall to the ground, and let us reach out to one another and to the world in our mutual need. For we are not without a balm for the bitter wound of loneliness. The mighty and eternal love of Christ has been revealed to us. We have a remedy for the world. We have an answer to the empty idols after which the world chases.

People: *The faith we have been given, the love we have known, the fellowship of the Spirit that is God's gift to us — these are to be shared* *with the world, to be given away to all who have yet to hear they are not alone.*

Leader: For have you not heard? Was it not told you from the beginning? Ask, and it shall be given. Seek, and you shall find. Knock, and the door will be opened. For the risen Christ walks by your side, stands at your right hand, abides with you in your journey. Lift up your needy soul to him who is the truth, and you will find the remedy for your isolation. Amen.

❧ the creation ❧

Leader: What mind could conceive of the fireflies drifting in the leafy branches of the cottonwood on a warm summer night? What heart could create the polar bear frolicking across the ice with her cubs? What hands could fashion the brave sparrow, the tiny wings of the hummingbird, and the mighty span of the eagle? Who shapes the snow-peaked mountains rising in majesty above the flowing plains whereon the antelope and deer find pasture? Who has set all of creation in delicate balance? Who calls the rain forth in due season and sends the warm winds of spring when it is time? Who plants the vast forests and sets a boundary to the mighty oceans?

People: *"Ever since the creation of the world God's eternal power and divine nature, invisible though they are, have been understood and seen through the things he has made."*[1]

Leader: We have seen the image of our home, hanging like a jewel against the darkness of the heavens: russet and amber, rose and green and blue, a sphere whose beauty alone speaks of grace.

People: *The one who came as a ransom for many came also to redeem the creation itself. The Christ came to restore the proper stewardship of Eden, the stewardship of tending and caring for the home God had created.*

Leader: Each day the forests retreat before the greed of humanity. Each day the streams and rivers and oceans groan as poisons are poured into them. Each day the earth's air becomes harder to breathe. Each day the blindness of human pride and arrogance threaten the delicate balance of creation.

People: *From the intricate architecture of the spider's web to the massive wake of the gray whale, from the forests rising on the mountainsides to the oceans teeming with life, the fragile loom of existence demands that humanity maintain its proper place within the balance.*

---

1. Romans 1:20.

Leader: O God, the beauty of your creation humbles us in wonder. We long to protect it, to nurture it, to tend it carefully as if it were Eden itself. Guide your people by your Holy Spirit into the paths of caring for the world you love. Inspire us to live on this lovely planet in harmony and peace with all that lives and breathes; in Jesus' name. Amen.

❧ the divine mystery ❧

Leader: God dances, and on earth lovers whisper to each other under the stars. The Holy One weeps, and the clouds water the fields of spring. The Creator laughs, and young sparrows fly up from the green shadows of summer. The Heavenly One prays, and somewhere on earth the word of forgiveness is spoken. The Spirit spins and weaves, brooding over the earth, and the people of God turn, shaping the architecture of their salvation. Summer turns to autumn, autumn to winter, and winter greets the spring as a young girl greets her beloved. The vast wheel of God's dream turns and moves, and we are caught up in a beauty and mystery beyond our understanding.

People: *Glory be to God in the highest, who alone does marvelous things, whose tender mercies we bear witness to. Spring is a bouquet prepared with infinite care; autumn a wild blaze of color like a gypsy's skirt. Winter is chaste and pure, and summer a full-throated song. In God's creation can be seen the revelation of divine perfection.*

Leader: "Behold!" says your God. "I am like a woman who has lost a precious coin. I have lit my lamp and swept every corner of heaven and earth, and I have found you, one who delights my heart even as a child lights up the face of her mother."

People: *God delivers us because God delights in us. All heaven sings because we have been found, we have been claimed, we have been chosen.*

Leader: Fire. Wind. Light. Father. Mother. In so many ways we try to name you, you who cannot be named. We would contain you, limit you with our words, you who cannot be contained, cannot be limited. Your overwhelming goodness fills heaven and earth. Our hearts overflow with joy, and when you draw near we can only exclaim:

All: *Come, Beloved One, come and rule within us. Come, O Love, and abide with us on our journey. Sing, Love, when we sing. Dance when we dance. Weep, Love, when we weep. And guide us, Love, all the days of our lives until you receive us into your tender, eternal embrace. Amen.*

litanies for
the church

❧ communion ☙

Leader: Have the angels not already been sent forth, and have we not been gathered here this morning from the ends of the earth? For we come from distant lands. We are different colors and speak different tongues. We are male and female, young and old, learned and unlettered, wealthy and poor, in joy and in pain, full of the Spirit and desirous of having our thirst quenched.

People: *For God said, "My house shall be called a house of prayer for all peoples."*[1]

Leader: Wherever gentleness dwells, wherever love reaches out to lift a sister in need or cradle a wounded brother, wherever people share their hearts honestly, either in joy or in pain, wherever kindness and compassion mingle with the sorrow of the world, wherever what is human is honored and respected and nurtured, there the Spirit of Christ dwells and is at work.

People: *We have a story to tell the nations, to share with the world, to give to our neighbors. It is the story of the victory of our God over sin and death, over fear and violence. It is the story of wounded love and final healing. It is our story and the story of humanity.*

Leader: O God, all around the world this day followers of your Son Jesus gather in holy communion, seeking empowerment to become instruments of your peace. Let that peace, that power, that love come upon your church this day.

People: *Let the unity of the Holy Spirit knit together the church of Christ in one seamless garment and joy and service. Let Christ's love prevail over discord and brokenness.*

Leader: For surely the time is at hand and our fulfillment in joy is at our very gate. Surely heaven draws close and Christ dwells within us and among us.

---

1. Isaiah 56:7.

People: *Hosanna in the highest to our God, even God who created heaven and earth and who alone is good.*

Leader: Lift up your hearts!

People: *We lift them up to God!*

Leader: Come to the feast, sons and daughters of the Most High! Come and taste the sweet fare your risen brother sets before you. Partake and rejoice, for your Savior dwells among you in perfect joy.

People: *Our hearts shall sing forever!*

Leader: This table is a table of joy. This feast is a feast of victory. This bread is the bread of healing. This cup is the cup of salvation.

People: *Renew your church, O God! Restore its ministries!*

Leader: Let all who come to the table receive what they need in good measure, pressed down, shaken together, running over.

People: *For our God is generous, slow to anger and abounding in steadfast love.*

Leader: God of Israel, behold and bless! See and rejoice! Hear and be glad! For your people are one people. Your sons and daughters are one family joined in the unity and equality of love. They are one even as you are one with your beloved child, even the one whose suffering has brought us peace.

All: *Christ our Passover has risen! Therefore, let us keep the feast! Amen.*

ministry of the laity

Leader: How beautiful the body of Christ! How lovely the people of God! Truly no gift has been withheld from God's servants. God, like a mother with her children, has showered down an equal love upon all. How gifted are the people of God, how special the gifts! Each servant holds a unique treasure for the world, each disciple bears a special flame to illuminate those who are encountered on his or her path. How beautiful the Spirit of God! How wise the Holy Spirit to call a whole people to the ministry of Christ, that none should be left idle by the vineyard but all employ their gifts to God's glory.

People: *The stole of our ordination is ours in the waters of our baptism.*

Leader: You are the altar itself of God's presence in the world, and your heart the holy chamber where Christ dwells.

People: *The mantle of our authority is bestowed upon us by the gentle love of Christ.*

Leader: Where you sing, where you dance, where you work, there Christ is present to the world, bringing joy and healing, strength and hope.

People: *The garments of our priesthood are given to us by Jesus himself, who calls each of us to go forth in the world to serve and minister as he did.*

Leader: Not a temple of stone and wood to which one might pilgrimage to see God's light, Christ himself was a light moving among the people, seeking them out where they worked and lived.

People: *So our light must not burn only in God's house, but move out into the world, into the halls of commerce and education and law, wherever our path might lead.*

Leader: For God cannot work apart from the people of God. Christ cannot embrace without our arms, cannot speak but with our voices, cannot illuminate but with the flame of our spirits.

People: *No dove descended at our baptism, no rending of the heavens greeted our ascent from the waters, but the light of resurrection rests upon us as a mantle of joy, a priestly cloak that gives our love authority and power.*

Leader: The Scripture the world needs lies in the countenance of joy and peace each of us takes outside these walls this morning. God's invitation to each of us is to become the word of God in the marketplace and in the schoolroom, in the law courts and in the streets.

All: *With joy let us accept Christ's gracious invitation. For each of us is gifted for our work. Let none stand idle, that the light of God's people and the light of Christ may be one light, burning as a beacon of love and hope so that the world's people might know how cherished they are in God's heart. Amen.*

church anniversary

Leader: Bricks, stone, steel, glass, wood that once sheltered birds and now shelters those more precious than birds; cloth and tapestry woven by hands veined with the hard lessons of love; light falling like the dew of Zion herself; children of God planted like green olive trees in the very sanctuary of God's heart; choirs lifting up God upon the praises of Israel, and words — words of wisdom, words of gentleness, words blazing, streaming, flowing like the Jordan in a flood of prophecy among the shining faces of a people saved and redeemed. Behold! This is house of God!

People: *We stand triumphant before our God. We stand unashamed because we have stood the test. The fire that glows in our midst is kindled still, and not one tiny ember has been lost along the way.*

Leader: Have you not heard? Was it not told you from the beginning? Have not the stars sung this truth to every generation, announced it to Abraham our father, poured down their light upon our Christ who came to us as a child? Have not the mountains trumpeted forth and the hills skipped like rams, the oceans roared and the rivers danced, the forests and the streams called out to flock and herd and all that lives and breathes: The Lord our God is one, a mighty God slow to anger and abounding in steadfast love whose arm is swift to save and who grows neither weary nor weak.

People: *Full of grace and truth, our God has dwelt among us, offering shelter. The light shines into the darkness, and the darkness has not overcome it.*

Leader: Years of faithfulness in a world of brokenness and struggle are as an eternity in the eyes of God.

People: *One day within the courts of God's house is to be preferred to ten thousand days among the tents of the wicked.*

Leader: For here the word of prophecy is spoken. Here we are named for whom we truly are.

People: *We are children of God, sons and daughters of the Most High, a royal priesthood of servant leaders and a colony of heaven ministering to a world crying out for healing.*

Leader: Raise high the roofbeam of God's house!

People: *Let her banners and pennants fly forever in the winds of grace!*

Leader: Lift up the citadel of our God!

All: *Let this royal ship of God's gospel sail forth without fear into the winds of change. Raise the sail of faith and cast away the anchor of doubt. For a child, in utter trust, sleeps in the stern, and we, God's worthy servants, are called to steer this gospel ship toward homeward ports. Amen.*

❧ the festival of marriage ❧

Leader: When love appears, it is like a river suddenly springing forth in a parched land. When love makes its entrance, two separate hearts entwine gracefully, like ivy around holly. When love casts its spell, two people behold their destiny in the eyes, the arms, the hearts of each other. When love proclaims its presence, it is like a fountain rising in the desert, and all the people come for refreshment and renewal in its life-giving waters.

People: *These children of heaven have found each other. Serious and joyful, trembling yet full of courage, they have come into our midst to proclaim the birth of love, the beginning of new life.*

Leader: For where once there were two, now there shall be one flesh.

People: *Hosanna in the highest to our God, and blessings without number on these two in our midst!*

Women: *Who is this that looks forth like the dawn, fair as the moon, bright as the sun, terrible as an army with banners? It is our sister, transfigured by love. She is a rose of Sharon, a lily of the valley.*

Men: *Who is this that has come up from the fields, come up with a shout from the pasturing of his flocks? It is our brother, radiant under the gaze of his betrothed, shining like the sun in the glow of her love.*

Leader: We shall dance around these lovers. We shall circle them with joy.

People: *We shall bedeck them with garlands. We shall cast flowers at their feet.*

Leader: Husband, behold your wife.

Bride: *My beloved is mine and I am his.* *

Leader: Wife, behold your husband.

---

*The couple may wish to speak words of their own choosing here.

Groom: *How sweet is your love, my sister, my bride! You have ravished my heart!**

Leader: For love is as strong as death, passion fierce as the grave. Its flashes are flashes of fire, a raging flame. Many waters cannot quench love, neither can floods drown it. If one offered for love all the wealth of his house, it would be utterly scorned.[1]

All: *Let the music begin! Let the wine pour forth! Let mirth and laughter reign! Let joy and thanksgiving flow among us like a river in flood! For love has been born. Two have become one, and heaven itself shall echo with our festive shouts!*

Leader: And the young rabbi stands at the edge of the wedding feast surrounded by his disciples yet somehow alone, set apart, watching the guests drink the water now turned into wine. Before him lies a journey that will take him to a distant city and a terrible death, yet peace rests upon him like a garment. A long and unknown journey lies before the two joined in holy union today, but the one who is the truth and the way and the resurrection and the life will travel with them every step down that long road, and stand at the end to receive them into eternal glory. Amen.

---

1. Song of Solomon 8:6–7.

❧ farewell and blessing ❧

Leader: In the kingdom of God no good-bye is forever. In the body of Christ we may go separate ways, but we are forever bonded in the love of the risen one. For those who walk in the Spirit are continually connected to one another regardless of distance and time.

People: *Today we bid you farewell and bless you from our hearts. You have shared the gospel journey with us for a while, and your presence in our midst has enriched our lives and strengthened our faith.*

Leader: You have been words of God to us, full of light and grace.

People: *You have shared in our joys and our sorrows as we have shared in yours. Precious memories of your smiles, your wisdom, and your humor will sustain us in your absence.*

Leader: Each time we think of you, each time a memory of you comes to mind, it will be as an unspoken prayer rising to bless you, protect you, and keep you wherever you are and whatever challenges you face.

People: *Wherever you go, whatever you face, the blessing of this church will rest upon you. You will never be forgotten among God's people.*

Leader: The winds of love that brought you to us will now bear you forth into the arms of love in a distant place. The love in which you have walked with us is a love that will never let you go. The love of God abides with you wherever you are and in whatever circumstances you find yourself.

People: *Therefore go forth from us in joy and peace, sure in the knowledge that God's love will follow you all the days of your life.*

Leader: We will hold you in our hearts and memories forever.

People: *The love you have found here awaits you with open arms in the destination toward which you are going.*

Leader: And may the Lord bless you and keep you. May the Lord make his face to shine upon you and be gracious to you. May the Lord lift up his countenance upon you and give you peace.[1] Amen.

---

1. Numbers 6:24–26.

✎ closing benediction ✎

Leader: No longer do we seek peace. Now we come bearing peace. In the rucksack over our shoulder are a hundred small packages, each carefully wrapped, each an eternity of peace, each to be given to a neighbor, a loved one, a stranger.

People: *How could peace dawn except by word of mouth?*

Leader: O people of God! We are too wealthy with God's gifts. We are burdened down with love. We stagger under our blessings. Grace upon grace pours down upon us in a cascading torrent of beauty and truth. We must give out of our bounty to our neighbors, to our loved ones, to anyone who crosses our path.

People: *We are restless and eager to give out of the riches of Christ's inheritance. We will find peace in giving to others and receiving from them. Each day shall be like Christmas Day.*

Leader: All over this land this morning, all over this world, God's people are moving out with rucksacks on their backs. Their steps guided by the Spirit, they have begun their journey. As they travel toward Love's home, they shall give all their packages away.

People: *We are ready, Lord. We have rested here this morning, and you have fed us with your presence. Now we are ready to seek you under the open sky, to search out your quarters, and to touch your flesh and gaze into your eyes.*

Leader: Our God awaits our coming with breathless anticipation. Our God needs our love and our company to heal the terrible wounds of combat. Love will receive you with gladness, people of God. Love will put you at ease and minister to you for your long journey. For the home of the One who is Peace, Beauty, and Truth is on the earth, and the world becomes smaller every day. Go forth, therefore, alert and watchful. In seeking the One who is Peace, give away your packages of peace to all you encounter along the way. Amen.